To Michael,

With best wishes from

Laura Thee

D1756409

Snapshots of Village Life
A Pictorial History of Betley, Balterley and Wrinehill

Laura Lee

Grosvenor House
Publishing Limited

All rights reserved
Copyright © Laura Lee, 2022

The right of Laura Lee to be identified as the author of this
work has been asserted in accordance with Section 78
of the Copyright, Designs and Patents Act 1988

The book cover is copyright to Laura Lee

This book is published by
Grosvenor House Publishing Ltd
Link House
140 The Broadway, Tolworth, Surrey, KT6 7HT.
www.grosvenorhousepublishing.co.uk

This book is sold subject to the conditions that it shall not, by way of
trade or otherwise, be lent, resold, hired out or otherwise circulated
without the author's or publisher's prior consent in any form of binding or
cover other than that in which it is published and
without a similar condition including this condition being imposed
on the subsequent purchaser.

A CIP record for this book
is available from the British Library

ISBN 978-1-80381-146-8

Acknowledgements

I would like to thank everyone who has kindly given permission for the use of pictures and text: Simon Barnes, Betley Parish News, Robert Bettley-Smith, Brampton Museum and Art Gallery, British Newspaper Archive, Nigel Brown, Alistair J. Chadwick, Griselda Garner, Mark Goodge, Gwyn Griffiths, Richard Head, David Ingham, Jemima Jones, Shirley Kennerley, Tony Moyes, Leslie Platt, Duncan Richardson, Mavis E. Smith, Staffordshire Past Track, The Sentinel/StokeOnTrentLive, University of London, Victoria and Albert Museum, William Salt Library.

Image credits have been included on the relevant pages.

Credit for front cover photo: © Duncan Richardson, http://www.aroundbetley.co.uk/.

Credit for back cover photo: Jemima Jones.

Contents

Balterley

Wrinehill

Ravenshall, Bowsey Wood and Heighley Castle

Foreword

This comprehensive collection of photographs with relevant comments produces a short history of Betley, Balterley and Wrinehill up to the present time.

Laura Lee has set a new standard in monitoring change in a concise and stylish manner. The book will appeal to a range of readers – those who are seeking a nostalgic view of an attractive parish and those who could use it as a starting point for studying different aspects of the past.

Laura, a new member of Betley Local History Society (BLHS), should be congratulated on creating a carefully referenced history, brought to life as a visual record for the next generation in this Jubilee year.

Mavis E. Smith

BLHS Vice-Chair, July 2022

Preface

This book originated from the local photographs and information that I began to publish on the Betley Local History Society (BLHS) Facebook page in March 2021. At that time, the country was in the grip of lockdown due to the COVID-19 pandemic and in-person gatherings were an impossibility for any organisation. The subsequent question was: how best to keep the history of Betley, Balterley and Wrinehill alive?

I decided to use the BLHS Facebook page to post information on various local topics, each with an accompanying photo, sometimes from the old 'picture postcard' days, sometimes more modern. The response appeared to be very positive and other people contributed additional facts, such as family connections to the places mentioned. The lockdown restrictions disappeared, but the posts continue through to 2022, when we have just celebrated the milestone of Queen Elizabeth II's Platinum Jubilee. I realised it had now been 38 years since the publication of 'Betley in Old Picture Postcards' in 1984 and wanted to mark the Jubilee with a new book that reflected some of the multifaceted changes around Betley, Balterley and Wrinehill since the turn of the millennium. History is constantly evolving, and we are all part of that history.

I hope you enjoy the book.

Laura Lee, July 2022

Aerial view of Betley

As far back as 1886, the North Staffordshire Naturalists' Field Club wrote that the houses in Betley generally did not follow any conventional design and had instead been built in the diverse styles characteristic of different periods in history, suiting a wide variety of individual tastes.

In this aerial photograph from 2022, the medieval church building, the Edwardian chapel building, timber-framed and Victorian buildings can all be seen, along with the 1950s/1960s East Lawns estate and the 1970s housing developments Ladygates and Betley Hall Gardens. The present village's appearance with 'houses strung out along the main road'[1] stems from Betley's status as a medieval borough, created in the 13th century.

Credit: Jefferson Air Photography, Chester

[1] Reproduced with permission from *A History of the County of Staffordshire XI: Audley, Keele and Trentham* Victoria County History, London, 2013. ©University of London.

1

Betley, Australia

The village of Betley shares its name with Betley, a rural locality in Victoria, Australia, 140km north-west of Melbourne, which had a recorded population of only 69 in 1954.

Originally known as Middle Bridge, the Australian Betley's name was adopted in 1910. It is reported that the inspiration may have been Betley in Staffordshire.

Coincidentally, this black and white picture postcard of Betley, Staffordshire was posted to Victoria a year later in 1911, telling the recipient that Betley was 'a real old English village – a delightful place, one you would like to see very much'.

Credit: Watkin family collection

Betley celebrates
Queen Victoria's Coronation

In July 1838, the Staffordshire Advertiser reported on the Betley festivities held to mark Queen Victoria's Coronation the previous month.

'*The morning was ushered in with the ringing of the bells, which continued at intervals the whole of the day. At 2 o'clock in the afternoon the working class were entertained at the different inns with a dinner of good roast beef, plum pudding, and a plentiful supply of vegetables etc. [...]*

After dinner, the health of the Queen [...] was drunk with boundless enthusiasm: also the Royal Family; George Tollet, Esq., and the Betley Hall Family; Francis Twemlow, Esq., and the Betley Court Family [...] Between 3 and 4 o'clock in the afternoon a procession was formed, consisting of a band of music, preceded by a beautiful ornamental crown, and followed by banners, on which were the letters "Long may Victoria reign", "The Queen, God bless her." [...]

The procession, which consisted of between [400] and 500 persons, halted opposite the mansions of Betley Court and Betley Hall, and sung [sic] the National Anthem [...]

In the evening, there was a dance upon the lawn at Betley Hall, which was tastefully laid out with bowers and ornamented with evergreens and flowers'.[1]

This postcard (postmarked 1931) includes pictures of Betley Hall and Betley Court, both of which would host a variety of local events over the rest of the 19th century.

Credit: Watkin family collection

[1] With thanks to the British Newspaper Archive (www.britishnewspaperarchive.co.uk)

Betley Butcher's Shop (now Pool Farm Vets)

Village butchers included Dick Prince, Don Hodgkinson, Ray Gibson and Kevin Thorley. Philip Herman recalls a story that Dick Prince used to recount:

'[...] Mrs Forster's story about the boy who ate some watercress from Cracow Moss which had not been thoroughly washed. The boy thus swallowed some frogspawn which eventually hatched in his stomach and subsequently produced a frog. In desperation, his parents took him to the butcher's shop where he was made to sit over a plate of sliced steak, so breathing in the vapours of the red raw meat [...] attracted by the chance of a meal, the frog hopped up the boy's throat and out on the plate'.[1]

Credit: Thompson, D.B. (2005) *The Legacy of 'The Tollets' Estate' in the Landscape of the Present-Day Village of Betley as reflected in the Sale of 1925*, Betley.

[1] Herman, P.H., ed. Thompson, D.B. (2000) *A Wartime Evacuee Returns to Betley.* Betley.

Betley Volunteer Fire Brigade

The Betley fire engine was gifted to the village in 1870 by Francis Stanier Broade, a Silverdale ironmaster who was a tenant of Betley Hall at the time, and subsequently the Fire Brigade's first captain. The horse-drawn fire engine was manned by village volunteers and kept in 'a specially constructed building which now forms part of Betley Hall Cottage'.[1] The horse which pulled the engine was kept in an adjacent field.

Back Row (L-R): Arthur Tomkinson, Wilmot Taylor, Thomas Dean, James Brassington (junior), Frank Grosvenor.

Front Row (L-R): George Lyth, James Brassington (senior), George Fletcher-Twemlow, John Wrench, Frank Blades and 'Taylor' Philips.

Credit: Bishop, J. and Thompson, D.B. (2001) Betley Local History Society Newsletter Volume 1: Issue 2. © Betley Local History Society, John Bishop and David Thompson.

---

[1] Bishop, J. and Thompson, D.B. (2001) Betley Local History Society Newsletter Volume 1: Issue 2. ©Betley Local History Society, John Bishop and David Thompson.

Betley Smithy

In this postcard, Wilmot Taylor the blacksmith stands outside his house and blacksmith's workshop with a walnut tree at the front of the picture. Wilmot Taylor was also an auxiliary fireman with the Betley Volunteer Fire Brigade and a bellringer at Betley Church.

The walnut tree was felled when Taylor had petrol pumps installed, but its former location is remembered today through the name of the neighbouring Walnut Cottage. The black and white timber-framed house became a red-brick house called Howard Place and the smithy became Betley Garage.

Credit: Watkin family collection

Betley Garage

Although Wilmot Taylor had founded Betley Garage, its longest-serving proprietor was Ernest Cyril Ambrose, (known as Cyril), who ran the business from 1955 until his death in 1998.

Under Cyril Ambrose, Betley Garage was open seven days a week selling petrol, new and second-hand cars and undertaking vehicle repairs. In addition to automotive supplies, Cyril Ambrose also sold ice lollies which were kept in a large chest freezer down a narrow passageway.

After Ambrose's death the petrol pumps were removed, and the building stood empty for a little while. Betley Garage and the adjacent house (Howard Place) were subsequently demolished in 2000 and the housing development Heighley Court was built on the site.

Credit: Watkin family collection

Betley Old Hall

Betley Old Hall dates from the mid to later 15th century and was most likely built for Ralph Egerton (died 1518).

The 17th century fireplace in the south room was decorated with a 'carved band of entwined hearts linked by rings that may have celebrated a marriage'[1] within the Egerton family.

It was extended and remodelled in the late 16th/early 17th centuries and became a Grade II* listed building in 1952.

By 1666, Randle Egerton had built a new house to the east of Betley Old Hall, and this became the first Betley Hall building which was sold to George Tollet I in 1718. The first Betley Hall was replaced with a red-brick Georgian mansion in 1783.

During the early 19th century, George Tollet IV of Betley Hall constructed a model farm 'mainly of orange-red brick but with some blue bricks and ashlar'[2] to the south-west of Betley Old Hall, comprising a water wheel as well as 'housing and stalls intended for over-wintering animals'.[3]

[1] Reproduced with permission from *A History of the County of Staffordshire XI: Audley, Keele and Trentham*. Victoria County History, London, 2013. ©University of London.
[2] Ibid
[3] Ibid

The model farm became Grade II* listed in 1988 and has subsequently been restored.

Credit: Watkin family collection

Betley Hall

Betley Hall was rebuilt in 1783 for Charles Tollet, a shipwright by trade. It was situated to the north of Betley, and the South Gates at the bottom of Church Lane (currently the Memorial Garden) opened on to a long tree-lined drive up to the Hall itself.

Betley Hall was described as having 'charming views over the park-like lands',[1] and when the Victorian author Elizabeth Gaskell visited the Hall in 1854, she complimented its charm but was 'confused about the address – "Betley Hall, Newcastle, although the hall is in Cheshire and the grounds in Shropshire"'.[2]

An interesting feature of Betley Hall in its later years was a Roman Catholic chapel, installed for Margaret MacDonald, who died in 1922.

Betley Hall and its estate (comprising many local properties and plots of land) were sold at auction in 1925 and 1947 and the Hall was subsequently demolished.

Credit: Watkin family collection

[1] Thompson, D.B. (2005) *The Legacy of 'The Tollets' Estate' in the Landscape of the Present-Day Village of Betley as reflected in the Sale of 1925.* Betley.
[2] Smith, M.E. (2005) *The Tollet Family of Betley Hall.* Betley.

Betley Hall Pool

The pool was originally a mill stream that marked the northern boundary of the parish and was part of a mill used for grinding corn until the mid-18th century.

The mill partially burned down in the 1760s and was subsequently demolished by George Tollet III, who had the mill stream converted into Betley Hall Pool.

The nine-year-old Florence Nightingale was taken boating on Betley Hall Pool in 1829 and commented on how delightful the experience was.

During the 1860s and 1870s, boating on the pool was also a feature of the annual festival of the Betley Friendly Society, held in the grounds of Betley Hall.

Betley Hall Pool is now situated at the bottom of the Betley Hall Gardens housing estate.

Credit: Watkin family collection

Betley Hall Hotel

Betley Hall Estate was sold in 1925 and a few years later the Hall was used as a country hotel.

In the late 1920s, there were a considerable number of newspaper advertisements for Betley Hall Hotel, which offered dances, tennis, boating and fancy-dress balls, in addition to stabling and a garage.

Betley Hall Hotel was marketed as the ideal place to spend Christmas and Whitsuntide (Pentecost) holidays. Guests could telephone 'Betley 8' to make a booking and a car was sent to meet guests' trains at the railway station.

Hotel managers included D.C. Mackenzie and M. Ellis.

DANCING & WHIST.

THE BETLEY HALL HOTEL. BETLEY.

POPULAR DANCES, from 9 to 2 a.m.
ARCADIAN REVELLERS' BAND.
Refreshments at Popular Prices. Special Buses.
MONDAY, JANUARY 11th.
FRIDAY, JANUARY 25th.
MONDAY, FEBRUARY 4th.
FRIDAY, FEBRUARY 15th.
MONDAY, FEBRUARY 25th.
FRIDAY, MARCH 8th.
2s. PER TICKET.
Or 10s. 6d. FOR THE SERIES OF SIX.
DANCE, BED and BREAKFAST. 9s.
'Phone Betley 8.
TEA DANCES, SUNDAY AFTERNOONS, 3 to 6.
2s. 6d. Inclusive.
See Posters.

Credit: British Newspaper Archive (www.britishnewspaperarchive.co.uk)

Ivydene Garage

Sid Keen purchased Ivydene during the Betley Hall Estate auction in 1925. The garage sold petrol from on-site pumps 'drawn from two underground tanks',[1] which were filled in after petrol sales ceased in 1986.

Petrol was sourced from the company Russian Oil Products (ROP) until the 1960s, and the cast iron ROP inspection covers in the ground gave access to the tanks.

Jim Carter ran the garage between the 1960s and 1980s while his wife Brenda ran a shop at the front of the house. For a while, the shop also included a post office under the jurisdiction of Wrinehill Post Office, run by Mr and Mrs Derek Reah.

John Seddon owned Ivydene until 2005 when Chamberlain Developments converted the site into a housing development, removing the ROP covers in the process.

[1] Turner, T. (2009) Betley Local History Society Newsletter Volume 8: Issue 1. ©Betley Local History Society and Tony Turner

However, John Seddon wrote into the contract that the covers must be re-installed on completion of the building works, preserving them for the present day.

Credit: Turner, T. (2009) Betley Local History Society Newsletter Volume 8: Issue 1. © Betley Local History Society and Tony Turner.

Ladygates

This pen and sepia drawing by Cornelius Varley depicts a view of St. Margaret's Church, Betley from the grounds of Betley Hall in 1820. The inhabitants of the Hall would have come down the Ladies' Walk and through the Lady Gates to get to church, which resulted in the name of the housing development 'Ladygates', built by Clarke's Quality Homes in the early 1970s.

The Betley Hall cellars were used during World War Two to provide Betley School pupils with shelter from daylight bombing raids, with the cellars being accessed via the Ladies' Walk.

Credit: © Trustees of the William Salt Library.

Betley Hall Gardens

In 1947, the Betley Hall Estate was put up for auction 'by order of the Executors of the late Hugh Woolf Esq'.[1] Prior to his death in an aeroplane crash, Hugh Woolf had been in the process of renovating Betley Hall.

Lot 1 in the auction included the walled garden, stables and centrally heated greenhouses containing grape vines, peaches, figs and tomatoes. Cyril Walton Ball bought Lot 1 in the 1947 auction and subsequently sold the land to Charles Edward (Ted) and Mary Fernihough. The Fernihoughs developed a market garden, growing cos lettuces, beans, tomatoes and a variety of flowers, as well as creating Christmas holly wreaths, assisted by their full-time gardener (Gordon Elkes). In the mid-1970s, the Fernihoughs sold the land to Clarke's Quality Homes, who had recently completed the Ladygates housing development. Clarke's subsequently built a second housing development: the present-day Betley Hall Gardens. Mr Fernihough died in 1982 and Mrs Fernihough in 2002.

Telephone: BETLEY 281

BETLEY HALL GARDENS

(Proprietor: C.E. FERNIHOUGH)

Bedding Plants etc.

Specialists in - TOMATO PLANTS - PANSIES - POLYANTHUS - CHRYSANTHEMUMS
BOUQUETS - SPRAYS - WREATHS.

Made to order

VISITORS WELCOME

Credit: © Betley Parish News.

---

[1] With thanks to the British Newspaper Archive (www.britishnewspaperarchive.co.uk)

The Betley Window

The Betley Window, or the Morris Dancers' Window, is believed to date from around 1550–1621. It was installed in the first Betley Hall (erected by the Egerton family), and later moved to the new Betley Hall (built in 1783) – by 1925 it had been installed in the Roman Catholic chapel there.

In the 18th century, the Hall's owner George Tollet III identified the figures in the Betley Window as (starting from the bottom left): 1) The Fool, 2) Maid Marian, Queen of the May, 3) The Friar, 4) Marian's Gentleman-Usher, 5) The Hobby-Horse, 6) The Clown, 7) A Gentleman of Fortune, 8) The Maypole, 9) Tom the Piper, 10) The Fleming, 11) The Spaniard, 12) The Counterfeit Fool.[1]

The Betley Window is now in the collection of the Victoria and Albert Museum, London. A copy was installed at Betley Court, unveiled by Viscount Bridgeman (a descendant of George Tollet IV of Betley Hall) and another in Kingston-upon-Thames, Surrey.

In 1981, the Post Office issued an 18p stamp featuring three of the figures in the Betley Window.

---

[1] Smith, M.E. (2005) *The Tollet Family of Betley Hall.* Betley.

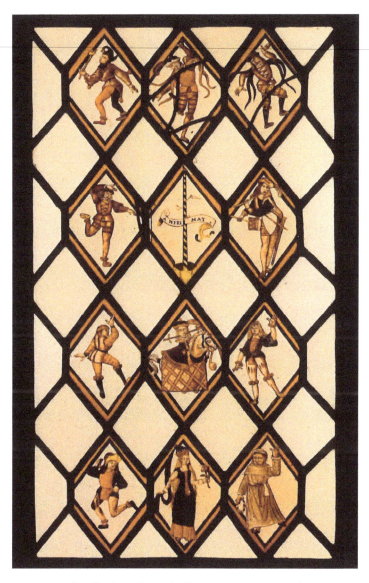

Credit: © Victoria and Albert Museum, London.

Betley greets King George V and Queen Mary

Main Road was bedecked with flags and bunting when King George V and Queen Mary (grandparents of Queen Elizabeth II) passed through Betley during their tour of North Staffordshire in April 1913. The Betley Hall Lodge and South Gates can be seen in the background.

However, the King and Queen weren't the only royals that Betley encountered during the early 20th century, as Grand Duke Michael Mikhailovich of Russia (second cousin to the last Russian Tsar Nicholas II) had opened Betley Show in 1903 and 1904. The Grand Duke was renting Keele Hall at the time and had been appointed Lord High Steward of Newcastle-under-Lyme. He had three children, one of whom (Nadejda) became aunt to Prince Philip, Duke of Edinburgh, husband of Queen Elizabeth II.

Credit: Brampton Museum and Art Gallery, Newcastle-under-Lyme Borough Council.

Betley Memorial Garden

Betley Memorial Garden is a piece of land on the site of the Betley Hall Lodge and South Gates. When the Lodge, South Gates and surrounding wall were demolished, Cyril Walton Ball (of Old Wood, Betley) gave the land to the village in 1971 in remembrance of his wife Kay, who died in 1969. A memorial plaque is located next to the notice board (see picture on next page), this commemorates Kay Ball.

Another plaque on the Memorial Garden commemorated the twinning of Betley with Agny, France in 1990, this has since been removed. Also, a bench was installed in memory of 'Cappie' Goodwin, who died in 1994.

A walnut tree was recently planted to commemorate the children evacuated to Betley during World War Two, as well as a tree to mark the 70th anniversary of Betley and Wrinehill Women's Institute (WI) in 2008. The original WI tree would later be joined by a replacement tree, planted in 2022.

Credit: Betley Memorial Garden © Duncan Richardson, http://www.aroundbetley.co.uk/.

Betley celebrates
Queen Elizabeth II's Platinum Jubilee

In 2022, Betley marked a significant historical occasion – the Platinum Jubilee of Queen Elizabeth II, who became the first British monarch to have reached such a milestone. An English Yew Tree (the Jubilee Yew – *Taxus baccata*) was planted on the Betley Memorial Garden, along with a Cypress Tree (the Memorial Cypress – *Cupressus macrocarpa* 'Goldcrest') in memory of the Queen's husband Prince Philip, Duke of Edinburgh, who had died the previous year. Each tree had a corresponding commemorative plaque.

Other village celebrations included a procession from the Memorial Garden to Betley Village Hall for an indoor picnic, led by a steam roller, a barbecue at The Swan Inn and the lighting of a beacon in a field above Betley Cricket Club.

Community celebrations for royal events have played key roles throughout Betley, Balterley and Wrinehill's history. In 1897, the Staffordshire Advertiser reported that 'upwards of a thousand persons partook of a good tea [in the grounds of Betley Court][1] to celebrate Queen Victoria's Diamond Jubilee.

Credit: Robert Bettley-Smith.

[1] With thanks to the British Newspaper Archive (www.britishnewspaperarchive.co.uk)

Betley fairs and markets

In 1227, King Henry III granted Henry de Audley a charter for a weekly market in Betley and a three-day fair 'upon the Eve, Day and Morrow after the feast of St. Margaret, July 20th'.[1] The market day was recorded as Tuesday by 1730, but the 1851 Staffordshire Directory noted that the market was held on Friday, and that there were also 'two fairs for cattle, etc. on July 31st and the last Tuesdays in April and October'.[2]

The market had ceased by the early 19th century, but the Betley Fair was still running in 1860.

Meanwhile, Betley Show was founded in 1857 and continues to the present day, held at Betley Court Farm.

[1] Fletcher-Twemlow, C. (1961) *The Betley Story: 1086–1961*. Betley.
[2] Ibid

The picture shows a copy of the proclamation which would have been read publicly at the start of the Betley Fair by the 'Mayor', who 'appears to have held office only for the duration of the fair'.[3]

PROCLAMATION OF BETLEY FAIR

OH, YES !   OH, YES !   OH, YES !

HEARKEN to The Queen's proclamation, and the Lord of this Manor, which willeth and strictly chargeth and commandeth, that no person or persons coming to this Fair, shall wear or bear any unlawful weapon to hinder or disturb any person or persons in the said Fair, or make any Affray, or cause any Bloodshed, under the several penalties hereafter mentioned:—

TO WIT :

For every Affray with Weapon and Bloodshed : Ten Shillings.

For every Affray with Weapon and no Bloodshed : Three Shillings and Fourpence.

For every Affray without Weapon and Bloodshed : Six Shillings and Eightpence.

For every Affray without Weapon and no Bloodshed : One Shilling.

And the party or parties so offending to be apprehended and kept in custody until they or every one of them pay their respective forfeiture ; and that all persons coming to this Fair with Cattle and other Goods to Sell, do repair to the Toll Book, and pay the several and accustomary Tolls ; otherwise to be amerced in the Toll of Burden — and this is, for every Penny, one Pound. And lastly, that all Persons coming to the Fair shall be freed from all arrests to be made by the Lord's Stewards ; and free come, and free go, behaving themselves well in the said Fair as they ought to do.

GOD BLESS THE QUEEN AND THE LORD OF THIS MANOR

Credit: Fletcher-Twemlow, C. (1961) *The Betley Story: 1086–1961* Betley.

---

[3] Ibid

The Swan Inn

The Swan has been an active pub in Betley for over 300 years, although it has not always been in the same location.

In the 17th century, several houses in the village were assessed for tax. One of these houses belonged to William Brittain and was the village inn, first known as The Swan (as of 1635) and later becoming The Black Horse. As well as being an inn, The Swan also hosted a variety of events during the 19th century, ranging from timber auctions to an inquest. Events currently held at The Swan include quiz nights, bingo and live music.

In 1920, the Staffordshire Advertiser described The Swan as 'one of the most popular and best patronised licensed houses in the district',[1] and it is still going strong over 100 years later.

Credit: Watkin family collection

---

[1] With thanks to the British Newspaper Archive (www.britishnewspaperarchive.co.uk)

The Black Horse Inn

The Black Horse Inn 'served [Betley] as a coaching inn since at least 1603'[1] and the pub's name may have derived from its position in the village.

The Betley Market was held on Main Road in front of The Black Horse, and Prof Godfrey Brown reported that a black horse was a symbol of the Roman god Mercury, 'the protector of markets and road travel'.[2]

One of the proprietors had been a butler at Betley Hall, serving 'milk from the Hall farm as well as ale'[3], and in 1947 the Betley Hall Estate auction was held at The Black Horse.

The Black Horse and its Stable Bar became a social hub in Betley, hosting events such as dances, auctions of promises (raising money for Betley Primary School) and meetings of various village organisations.

[1] Herman, P.H., ed. Thompson, D.B. (2000) *A Wartime Evacuee Returns to Betley.* Betley.
[2] Brown, G.N. (1985) *Betley through the Ages.* Betley.
[3] Ibid

In 2000, The Black Horse was converted into three houses (Byrne Cottage, Black Horse House and Black Horse Cottage) and the housing development Chamberlain Court was constructed on the site of the pub car park/beer garden.

Credit: Watkin family collection

Betley celebrates the
50th Anniversary of VE Day

In May 1995, Betley joined in the national celebrations marking the 50th anniversary of Victory in Europe (VE) Day – the end of World War Two in Europe.

The celebrations included a parade of period military and civilian vehicles on Main Road, a 1940s 'Big Band' dance and a 'Betley in wartime' exhibition.

Crowds gathered outside The Black Horse Inn on Bank Holiday Monday to watch a Spitfire flypast (one of very few taking place in the country), followed by a children's tea party organised by three local groups – the WI, Playgroup and Betley Primary School's Parents and Teachers Association (PTA).

Children were also entertained with a puppet show in The Black Horse Inn following the tea party.

Credit: Watkin family collection

St. Margaret's Church, Betley

St. Margaret's Church, previously dedicated to the Virgin Mary, was originally a chapel of ease for Audley Church until 'a curacy was endowed [in Betley] in the early 17th century'.[1] Chapels of ease were built for communities who could not reach the parish church conveniently.

Betley Church underwent significant restorations in 1842 under W.B. Moffatt and George Gilbert Scott when 'the north and south aisles were widened and the chancel arch removed, although the distinctive late medieval timber-framing was preserved'.[2] (George Gilbert Scott was related to Giles Gilbert Scott, designer of the red telephone boxes).

[1] Reproduced with permission from *A History of the County of Staffordshire XI: Audley, Keele and Trentham* Victoria County History, London, 2013. ©University of London.
[2] Ibid

This postcard from 1904 shows the church decorated for Harvest Festival. Betley Church was noted for its elegant floral decorations at harvest time, with the chancel flowers being arranged by the Betley Court gardeners during the early 20th century.

Credit: Watkin family collection

Betley Methodist Chapel

In September 2003, Betley Methodist Chapel celebrated its centenary. The Edwardian building replaced an earlier (1808) Wesleyan Methodist chapel in the village and had a seating capacity of 150.

By the 1980s the building was becoming dilapidated, and the congregation had been 'forced to move out of the chapel'[1] into the Sunday School room because they were unable to afford the necessary repair costs.

In 1994, Newcastle-under-Lyme Borough Council approved plans by the Beth Johnson Housing Association to convert the chapel into five flats, now known as Wesley Court.

The former Sunday School room was refurnished and converted into a new chapel which opened in June 1998.

[1] With thanks to the British Newspaper Archive (www.britishnewspaperarchive.co.uk)

Methodism was also active elsewhere in the local area, with another Wesleyan Methodist chapel at Bowsey Wood (which closed in 1940) and a Primitive Methodist chapel on Den Lane, Wrinehill (which closed in 1969).

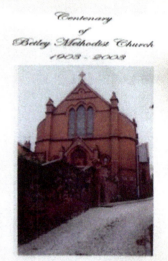

The present Chapel was Betley's second Methodist Chapel the first having been built in 1808. In 1898 Betley became part of the Nantwich Circuit Extension Scheme and was the sixth of a group of new country chapels erected in a similar mock Gothic style and built of Ruabon brick. The land was bought from Mr Samuel Shufflebotham. The foundation stone was laid in September 1902.

During 1997-1998 the Beth Johnson Housing Association converted the main building into flats while providing the Methodists with a newly refurbished Chapel in the original Sunday School room. A Service of Rededication was conducted by Rev. Bill Seville on Sunday 31st May 1998. The present Minister is Rev. Andrew Gunstone BA.

A friendly welcome awaits worshippers on Sunday's and partakers of "Coffee and Chat" on Wednesdays.

"Then let us adore and give Him His right
All glory and power; all wisdom and might;
All honour and blessing, with angels above
And thanks never ceasing; and infinite love".
Charles Wesley.

Centenary of Betley Methodist Church 1903 - 2003

PROGRAMME OF SPECIAL SERVICES during September 2003

Credit: Watkin family collection

Betley Court

Betley Court was built for John Cradock in 1716, who left two daughters (Anastasia and Catherine) as his heirs. Anastasia married John Fenton of Newcastle-under-Lyme and Catherine married Charles Tollet of Betley Hall. When the widowed Anastasia retired to Betley Court from Newcastle, she was 'troubled by the unreasonable activities of her brother-in-law Charles [...], who amongst other annoyances seems to have engineered her election as a churchwarden'.[1]

In the 1780s, Anastasia Fenton not only commissioned significant alterations to the house, but also engaged William Emes to replan the Betley Court grounds.

The Fletcher-Twemlow family lived at Betley Court from the 19th century until 1940, when the building was requisitioned as a Red Cross hospital (and later a rehabilitation centre). The family subsequently moved to Doddlespool Hall.

After the rehabilitation centre closed in 1965, Betley Court began to fall into disrepair until it was rescued by Prof Godfrey and Dr Freda Brown, who converted the house into flats.

---

[1] Reproduced with permission from *A History of the County of Staffordshire XI: Audley, Keele and Trentham* Victoria County History, London, 2013. ©University of London.

Restoration work on Betley Court is currently underway following the fire of 2019 which severely damaged the main house, along with 11 of the 14 flats.

Credit: Watkin family collection

Betley Mere

In 1851, White's History, Gazetteer and Directory of Staffordshire noted that the boundary line between Staffordshire and Cheshire extended through Betley Mere, which boasted abundant quantities of fish, some weighing 30lbs. A 'great mere'[1] at Betley was first mentioned in the 13th century and had become known as Betley Mere by the early 15th century.

Betley Mere previously belonged to the Egertons (later Earls of Wilton) of Wrinehill Hall, even when the land bordering the mere on the Betley side became part of the Betley Court grounds. Francis Twemlow of Betley Court became 'the Earl [of Wilton]'s tenant, paying a rent for the mere itself, together with fishing and shooting rights'.[2]

---

[1] Reproduced with permission from *A History of the County of Staffordshire XI: Audley, Keele and Trentham* Victoria County History, London, 2013. ©University of London.
[2] Ibid

Swimming races were held in Betley Mere throughout the 19th and early 20th centuries, including one celebrating Queen Victoria's Golden Jubilee in 1887.

Betley Mere is a Site of Special Scientific Interest (SSSI) due to its notable flora, fauna and wildlife habitats.

Credit: © Duncan Richardson, http://www.aroundbetley.co.uk/.

The Wilderness

The avenue of lime trees along Main Road is known as the Wilderness, and their aesthetic appearance evoked descriptions of the trees raising their 'tall, picturesque heads over the cottages as though asking a blessing [...] grand monuments to nature's most noble architecture'.[1]

The Wilderness was referenced as early as 1744 when it was noted that a row of lime trees stood in a direct line from John Cradock's malt kiln to his house (Betley Court).

Although half of the lime trees were situated within Betley Court gardens, the limes on the other side of the road stood on Lord Chetwynd's uncultivated land and had been planted there on his instructions. In John Cradock's time, the lime trees were closely clipped in the style of French château gardens, however the practice was discontinued.

[1] Fletcher-Twemlow, C. (1961), The Betley Story: 1086–1961, Betley.

Although several of the trees have now been felled, the Wilderness still maintains a striking presence in the village.

Credit: Watkin family collection

Betley Bonfire

Betley has included bonfires in many of its village celebrations over the years, such as those for the Coronations of George IV (1821) and Edward VII (1902). However, the present-day Betley Bonfire was first started by the Village Hall Committee, who in the early 1960s were raising funds for a new village hall in Betley (this opened in 1965). May Mottram made the Betley Bonfire 'Guy' for many years.

In 1961, it was reported that there were 100 guineas' worth of fireworks and aerial effects including 'Niagara Falls, a fantail pigeon, a palm court fountain, revolving suns and a St. Andrew's Cross'.[1]

The bonfire and fireworks display continues to attract crowds of visitors and was advertised in 2021 as one of the largest and best-known displays in the area.

Credit: ©The Sentinel/StokeOnTrentLive.

---

[1] With thanks to the British Newspaper Archive (www.britishnewspaperarchive.co.uk)

Betley Primary School

The first historical record of a school in Betley dates back to 1690, when the schoolhouse 'adjoined the curate's house next to the church'.[1] In 1826, the school was moved to a new building (the current Reading Room) and became Betley National School, as it was 'affiliated to the National Society'.[2] The National Society was founded in 1811 as *The National Society for Promoting the Education of the Poor in the Principles of the Established Church in England and Wales.*

However, the present Betley Primary School building dates from the Victorian era and was built on land given by George Tollet IV of Betley Hall in 1853. The building originally had separate schools for boys, girls and infants, but the boys' and girls' schools were combined in the early 20th century.

Betley School taught pupils up to the age of 14 years until educational reforms resulted in the age limit being capped at 11, and in 1957 all Betley pupils between 11–14 years of age moved to secondary schools.

[1] Reproduced with permission from *A History of the County of Staffordshire XI: Audley, Keele and Trentham* Victoria County History, London, 2013. ©University of London.
[2] Ibid

When the school closed for refurbishments in the 1990s, classes were taught in Betley Village Hall.

Credit: Betley Local History Society/Shirley Kennerley

Betley Ladies' College

In the 1830s, a boarding school for girls was founded at Grove House in The Butts, Betley, and by 1851 14 pupils (including one boy) were registered. Jane and Caroline Ratcliffe were named as the Principals.

By 1881 the school was run by Miss Anna Remer and her younger sister Ellen, who bought Prospect House as the new school building in 1889 after Anna Remer left to get married. The school was now known as Betley Ladies' College and offered optional subjects of German, Latin, advanced maths, painting, dancing, harmony and fencing, in addition to the usual curriculum.

References given in the school's prospectus included Mrs Twemlow of Betley Court, Revd Robert Boughey (Vicar of Betley) and Sir Delves and Lady Broughton of Doddington Hall. Ellen Remer died in 1910 and Betley Ladies' College closed in 1914.

This postcard shows an outdoor painting class at Betley Ladies' College in around 1900.

Credit: https://postcardsfromstoke.wordpress.com.

Betley Village Hall

Betley Village Hall was built on a plot of land gifted by the Fletcher-Twemlow family of Betley Court and was opened in 1965 by Major H.A. Hawkins (Chairman of the Staffordshire Education Committee). The dedication ceremony was performed by the Bishop of Stafford and the Superintendent Minister of the local Methodist Circuit. Prior to the opening of the village hall, some Betley events and group meetings had been held at Betley Church Hall, which was 'converted in 1930 from the disused Methodist chapel [separate to the present chapel] and sold in 1967'.[1]

Betley Village Hall is managed by a group of trustees and has become a long-standing meeting place for many village organisations, such as the Women's Institute and the Betley Amateur Theatrical Society (BATS).

In 1987, land next to the village hall was developed for use as a tennis court, followed by a bowling green in 1992.

---

[1] Reproduced with permission from *A History of the County of Staffordshire XI: Audley, Keele and Trentham* Victoria County History, London, 2013. ©University of London.

The refurbished village hall playground and new boules court were opened in 2019.

Credit: © Trustees of Betley Village Hall.

Betley Co-op

In February 1916, the Betley branch (No 22) of the Crewe Co-operative Friendly Society opened in front of the former Betley Ladies' College (The Croft/Prospect House). Some of the former college areas (such as the Headmistress' office) became stock rooms for the new Co-op.

Staff over the years included Connla and Barbara Lightfoot, Eddie Hodson (Manager), Roy Tew and Bill Ball.

The two houses to the right of the store were rented from the Co-operative Friendly Society and therefore became known as Co-op Cottages.

Betley Co-op closed in March 1968 and GB Engineering Services occupied the vacant building until 2005. The building was demolished three years later.

The photograph shows Connla Lightfoot and Eddie Hodson outside the Betley Co-op in 1963.

Credit: Tuttle, M. (2009) Betley Local History Society Newsletter Volume 8: Issue 2. ©Betley Local History Society and Mike Tuttle.

Hall o' the Wood

Hall o' the Wood (formerly known as Hallawood) was probably created by the lawyer George Wood, who died in 1558.

The present timber-framed house with its decorative framing is believed to have been commissioned in the 17th century by William Lawton, who sold it to Richard Kelsall of Halmer End.

William Kelsall of Hall o' the Wood established a free school at Balterley Green in the 18th century and left instructions 'that his heir pay a £2 salary to the mistress, Martha Bowler'.[1] However, the ensuing history of the school is unknown.

In 1843, the house was 'set in pleasure grounds within a 91 [acre] estate'.[2]

---

[1] Reproduced with permission from *A History of the County of Staffordshire XI: Audley, Keele and Trentham* Victoria County History, London, 2013. ©University of London.
[2] Ibid

Hall o' the Wood was held by trustees between 1858 and 1906, when it was sold to Eliza Fletcher-Twemlow of Betley Court. The house became a Grade II* listed building in 1952.

Credit: H. Saunderson https://britishlistedbuildings.co.uk/.

All Saints' Church, Balterley

All Saints' Church, Balterley sits within the Diocese of Chester, unlike its neighbouring Betley Church which belongs to the Diocese of Lichfield.

Eliza Fletcher-Twemlow founded Balterley Church in 1900 in memory of her husband Thomas Fletcher-Twemlow of Betley Court, who died in 1894.

The Rectors of Barthomley Church had pastoral oversight of Balterley, and included James Skene, James Bennett and Steve Collis.

The red brick and sandstone building, designed by the architects Paley and Austin of Lancaster, was consecrated in 1901, and became a Grade II listed building in 1988.

Church services were discontinued at All Saints' Church in 1995 but resumed three years later, continuing until the church closed in 2019. The building was subsequently put up for sale and is now believed to have been sold.

Credit: By Jonathan Billinger CC BY-SA 2.0 https://commons.wikimedia.org/w/index.php?curid=7999584

Balterley Hall

Balterley Hall was historically the home of the Thicknesse family, who had a family chapel in Betley Church. In 1320, the owner of the Hall was William de Thicknesse, coroner of Staffordshire and twice mayor of Newcastle-under-Lyme. Ralph Thicknesse sold the estate in 1790 to Revd Joseph Crewe, whose son John sold it to Thomas Twemlow (father of Francis Twemlow of Betley Court) and his brother George.

The current Hall dates from the early 18th century and a south wing was added to the building in 1870. Balterley Hall remained in the Twemlow family until it was sold to the Edwards family in the 1980s, and subsequently to David Beecroft in 2000.

Balterley Hall became a Grade II listed building in 1952, and the barns to the south of the house were converted into houses in the early 21st century (becoming known as Balterley Court).

Credit: Balterley Hall c/o Bespoke Lettings Ltd.

Betley Road station

Betley Road station was built in 1875 on the London and North Western Railway line between Stafford and Crewe (now known as the West Coast Main Line) and was opened shortly before the line was quadrupled to 'cope with the expanding volume of both passenger and goods traffic'.[1] It consisted of four canopied platforms, and the station facilities included waiting rooms, a weigh bridge and a slot machine selling bars of Nestlé's milk chocolate for 1d (old penny).

Despite its name, Betley Road station was in fact situated on Station Road (now Den Lane) in Wrinehill. Rural stations were sometimes located 'several miles away'[2] from the communities they were built to serve, as the railway proprietors' primary concern was to 'find the easiest route for their tracks and locomotives rather than to link up the centre of the village communities'.[3] In these cases, the word 'Road' would be added to the station name, resulting in Betley Road.

---

[1] Thompson, D.B. (2002) The Railway and Railwaymen of Betley, Betley Local History Society, Occ. Pub No 2.
[2] Forster, H. and H. (2001) Betley Road station and Betley Road tip.
[3] Ibid

Betley Road station closed to passengers in 1945 and to goods traffic in 1950.

Credit: Betley Local History Society.

This picture shows a third-class daily return ticket from Betley Road to Madeley, dated September 1929.

Credit: Betley Local History Society.

Betley Road signal box

The Betley Road signal box survived for more than 50 years after Betley Road station had closed and 45 years after its neighbouring Wrinehill signal box had been dismantled.

Betley Road signal box played a prominent role in railway operations both before and after the station's closure, controlling in its heyday 'some 12 main line signals as well as several complicated points and crossings'.[1]

It had become one of the longest serving signal boxes on the West Coast Main Line when it closed in June 2004.

[1] Forster, H. and H. (2001) Betley Road station and Betley Road tip.

The signal box top was subsequently moved to Northampton and Lamport Railway.

Credit: Betley Road signal box (exterior) – David A. Ingham.

This picture shows the interior of Betley Road signal box shortly before its closure.

Credit: Betley Road signal box (interior) – Simon Barnes.

Wrinehill Post Office

Wrinehill Post Office was originally situated on New Road, with proprietors including Clifford and Vicky Johnson and Mr and Mrs Derek Reah.

Wrinehill Post Office was the first business in Betley and Wrinehill to sell petrol and have a petrol pump installed. It was referred to as a 'veritable social centre, replete with the smells of coffee grinding and the charging of accumulators'.[1]

The New Road site closed in 1990 and Mrs Pamela Lane ran Wrinehill Post Office from the former GP surgery (now a private residence) in Ravenshall until 1993, when the post office became incorporated into Betley Village Shop.

In this postcard, Wrinehill Primitive Methodist Chapel can be seen in the background at the end of Station Road/Den Lane.

Credit: Watkin family collection

[1] Herman, P.H., ed. Thompson, D.B. (2000) *A Wartime Evacuee Returns to Betley.* Betley.

The Blue Bell Inn

The Blue Bell Inn, situated on New Road, Wrinehill, was constructed in mind to facilitate the turning of carts and wagons from Checkley Lane onto New Road and vice versa.

The first publican was Hugh Whittacker in the 18th century, and other publicans included Richard and Mary Sherwin, Thomas Harding and Ernest Hardern.

The Blue Bell Inn had an adjacent bakehouse (formerly a stable), which was demolished in 1974 (along with another house next door) to make room for the pub car park. There was also a shop located inside the inn which sold paraffin and groceries.

The original Wrinehill Upper Gate toll board was displayed at The Blue Bell Inn for many years and is now in the collection of the Brampton Museum, Newcastle-under-Lyme.

After The Blue Bell Inn was demolished around 2013, the site was developed for housing and is now known as Blue Bell Close.

Credit: User: Peter Morrell, CC BY 3.0 <https://creativecommons.org/licenses/by/3.0>, via Wikimedia Commons

Wrinehill Upper Gate toll board

The toll road system has been in existence for a few thousand years, but the major toll roads in England and Wales were established 'sometime after 1706'.[1]

Turnpike Trusts (groups of businesspeople and local gentry) set the toll charges. In the days when people and goods were transported by horse and cart, 'wear on the road surfaces was considerable'.[2] Carriages or wagons that had broad wheels and caused less wear to the road surface could therefore receive a discount.

In 1830, a new road on the Newcastle–Nantwich route was laid out in Wrinehill to 'avoid the steep rise of the old line of the road (now Old Road) behind [the] Summer House'.[3] Wrinehill subsequently had an upper and lower toll gate – the upper at The Blue Bell Inn, facing the Checkley Lane junction, and the lower was next to The Hand and Trumpet Inn.

It was reported that the toll board displayed at The Blue Bell Inn was 'probably the last one to be used, since it refers to the toll charges made in 1822 and 1829'.[4] The toll board would have been affixed to the Wrinehill Upper Toll House, opposite The Blue Bell Inn.

Tolls along the Newcastle–Nantwich turnpike road were discontinued in 1877.

[1] Smith, M.E. (2009) Betley Local History Society Newsletter Volume 8: Issue 2. ©Betley Local History Society and Mavis E. Smith.
[2] Ibid
[3] Reproduced with permission from *A History of the County of Staffordshire XI: Audley, Keele and Trentham* Victoria County History, London, 2013. ©University of London.
[4] Smith, M.E. (2009) Betley Local History Society Newsletter Volume 8: Issue 2. ©Betley Local History Society and Mavis E. Smith.

This picture shows the Betley Local History Society's copy of the Wrinehill Upper Gate toll board.

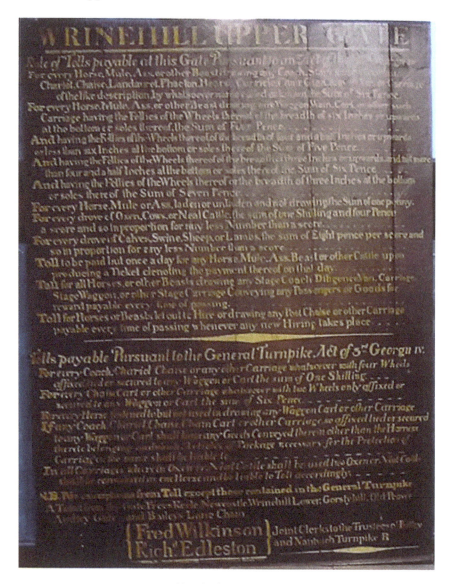

Credit: Shirley Kennerley.

The Red Lion Inn

The Staffordshire Advertiser reported several antisocial incidents at The Red Lion Inn, Wrinehill during the 19th century.

In 1841, thieves broke into The Red Lion 'by way of the cellar, but [...] being disturbed, decamped, taking with them only a bottle of gin'.[1] There were also reports of publicans 'keeping open [the] premises at illegal hours'[2] and a customer refusing to leave the pub when requested to do so by Mrs Blagg the landlady.

The Red Lion Inn subsequently became the Medicine House in 1880, so called because the apothecary Samuel Johnson used the building to make up his Staffordshire Cure-All Medicine. Johnson's XX Staffordshire Cure-All Pills were also sold over the counter at Wrinehill Post Office.

---

[1] With thanks to the British Newspaper Archive (www.britishnewspaperarchive.co.uk)
[2] Ibid

The Medicine House was removed in 1970 to its present site in Blackden, Cheshire and is now owned by the Blackden Trust, co-founded by author Alan Garner and his wife Griselda in 2004.

Credit: The Blackden Trust.

The Summer House

The Summer House in Wrinehill was built around 1710–1720 for Sir John Egerton and is mainly constructed of red Flemish bond brickwork. Its internal features included an oak staircase with spiral banisters.

The Egertons lived at Wrinehill Hall, and the Summer House commanded good views of the Hall parkland. Throughout its history the building has had various functions, including use as a barracks and a shop.

Samuel Johnson (of Staffordshire Cure-All fame) was the tenant there from 1869, and its owner from 1918. He conducted his apothecary business from the Summer House, which was depicted on the company's ointment pots.

After Samuel Johnson's death in 1921, his family continued the business until the late 1960s. The Summer House became a Grade II* listed building in 1952.

Credit: By Peter Styles, CC BY-SA 2.0, https://commons.wikimedia.org/wiki/File:The_Summer_House_on_Main_Road,_Wrinehill,_Staffordshire.jpg.

Wrinehill Hall

Wrinehill Hall was the home of the Egerton family, who later moved to Tatton Park, Cheshire.

The original house stood on a moated site mentioned in the 1540s, although there may have been a hunting park at Wrinehill as early as 1300.

In 1754, the area then known as the 'Old Park' lay to the south of Wrinehill Hall's formal gardens.

The Hall was rebuilt in the early 17th century for Sir John Egerton and was depicted in a 1725 drawing as a two-storey, H-shaped house which overlooked a courtyard. Although Wrinehill Hall had been demolished by 1754, the formal garden still existed, comprising a walled area with two iron gates enclosing eight grass plots. The plots were bordered with shrubs and had a long water feature on the south side (probably known as the 'Great Pool'). There was also a rectangular fish pond to the north at the corner of the orchard, and breeding carp were purchased for Wrinehill Hall in the 17th century. Carp is still fished from Wrinehill Pool (pictured) to this day.

Credit: Leslie Platt.

Sergent's Garage

Charles Sergent, a Frenchman, first came to the area as a batman to Major Hugh Dodds CMG, who changed his name to Crewe in 1945. Major Dodds was the husband of Lady Annabel Crewe-Milnes of Madeley Manor and Crewe Hall, and father of the author/restaurateur Quentin Crewe.

Sergent married Margaret Sutton of Madeley and worked as Lady Annabel's chauffeur before starting a coach business and small garage in the former smithy at Wrinehill in 1950. The business was 'housed in a large corrugated-steel shed which had a substantial clock mounted on its gable end'[1] and ran school and works bus services along with a market day public service to Nantwich via Checkley and Hunsterson.

The precise date when the business closed is unclear but appears to have been around 1985, although the Nantwich service would have been withdrawn at an earlier date.

[1] Herman, P.H., ed. Thompson, D.B. (2000) *A Wartime Evacuee Returns to Betley.* Betley.

This photograph was taken at Sergent's in September 1972 and shows a Leyland Titan bus (registration: LFS 462) which ran a works service to Rists in Newcastle-under-Lyme and a Bristol LS6G bus (registration: XNU 420).

Credit: A. Moyes.

The Lord Nelson Inn

The Lord Nelson Inn, Wrinehill was formerly owned by the Earl of Wilton and was demolished in 1962. It was located on a site that eventually became 'the car showroom of Wrinehill Garage'[1] (run by Albert Austin until 2004).

Publicans included William and Elizabeth Summerfield, Joseph Bailey and Harry Dale.

The Lord Nelson publicans also ran the on-site smithy (which later became Sergent's Garage) until about 1881. The brewery Woolf's (named on the pub building) was based at Wistaston Road, Crewe and closed in 1923.

[1] Herman, P.H., ed. Thompson, D.B. (2000) *A Wartime Evacuee Returns to Betley.* Betley.

In this postcard, The Blue Bell Inn can be seen in the background.

The Lord Nelson Inn benefitted from its Staffordshire location, which allowed it to stay open until 10.30pm, whilst The Blue Bell Inn was in Cheshire – and consequently had to close at 10.00pm. Changes to the county boundary lines in the 1960s saw The Blue Bell Inn's location become part of Staffordshire.

Credit: https://postcardsfromstoke.wordpress.com.

Ravenshall

Ravenshall, a hamlet on Main Road between Wrinehill and Betley, has been known by several different names over the centuries, including Randall, Rensall and Ravenshollow. It has also been noted that the name is a corruption of Ranehollow, meaning 'hollow lands under the boundary'.

In 1327, Stephen de Ravenshollow was named in the Subsidy Rolls of Betley – he had taken his surname from his place of residence. At this time, Ravenshall also 'had its own open fields, implying a separate community from Betley'.[1]

Ravenshall Farm and Ravenshall House were both assessed for tax on hearths in 1666 and today Ravenshall contains 'some of the oldest surviving houses in the parish'.[2]

Credit: https://postcardsfromstoke.wordpress.com.

[1] Reproduced with permission from *A History of the County of Staffordshire XI: Audley, Keele and Trentham* Victoria County History, London, 2013. ©University of London.
[2] Ibid

Bowsey Wood

The name Bowsey derives from an Old English word 'bosig', meaning 'a stall for animals, especially cows, and suggests that the wood was valued for its pasture'.[1]

Bowsey Wood had its own water wheel mill fed by water from Checkley Brook (which also supplied the mill at Wrinehill), but the mill closed in 1939 when its machinery was taken to assist the war effort during World War Two.

Bowsey Wood mill formed part of the 304-acre estate in Betley that was sold to George Tollet I in 1718, along with 307 acres in Audley. However, there are noted contradictions relating to the ownership of Bowsey Wood mill during the 18th century. John Cradock of Betley Court was also reported to have owned the mill and subsequently 'interfered with the water supply to Wrinehill mill, allegedly as a means of getting at its owner Sir John Egerton with whom he was in dispute about access to a pew in Betley Church'.[2]

[1] Reproduced with permission from *A History of the County of Staffordshire XI: Audley, Keele and Trentham* Victoria County History, London, 2013. ©University of London.
[2] Ibid

The remains of Bowsey Wood mill can be seen in the photograph. Bowsey Wood's Wesleyan Methodist chapel (built in 1833 and closed in 1940) is now a private residence.

Credit: Tuttle, M. (2010) Betley Local History Society Newsletter Volume 9: Issue 2. ©Betley Local History Society and Mike Tuttle.

Heighley Castle

Heighley Castle was built as a hilltop fortress by Henry de Audley around 1220. The lords of Audley acquired the manor of Betley in the 13th century and were subsequently granted 'market and fair rights'[1]. The Audleys also had residences at Red Castle (Hawkstone, Shropshire), Buglawton Manor (Congleton) and Newhall Tower (Combermere, Cheshire).

The castle commanded extensive views, particularly towards Henry de Audley's Shropshire estates. It was surrounded by a park, for which a royal grant of deer was made in 1222. The park, which 'stretched eastwards up to the Madeley parish boundary'[2] was maintained by four gatekeepers in 1299.

During the English Civil War (1642–1651), the Parliamentary Committee at Stafford ordered the demolition of Heighley Castle, as they feared that it could be used as a stronghold for Royalist forces.

---

[1] Reproduced with permission from *A History of the County of Staffordshire XI: Audley, Keele and Trentham* Victoria County History, London, 2013. ©University of London.
[2] Ibid

The castle ruins were granted Grade II listed building status in 1966 and Heighley Castle is a scheduled ancient monument.

Credit: Staffordshire Past Track/Staffordshire County Council.

Lightning Source UK Ltd.
Milton Keynes UK
UKHW020733090223
416624UK00001B/70

9 781803 811468